Anonymous

200th Anniversary of the Clinton Congregational Church

Anonymous

200th Anniversary of the Clinton Congregational Church

ISBN/EAN: 9783337235994

Printed in Europe, USA, Canada, Australia, Japan

Cover: Foto ©Lupo / pixelio.de

More available books at **www.hansebooks.com**

TWO HUNDREDTH

ANNIVERSARY

OF THE

Clinton Congregational Church,

HELD IN

CLINTON, CONN.,

November 13th, 1867.

NEW HAVEN:

TUTTLE, MOREHOUSE & TAYLOR, STEAM PRINTERS.

- - - - - - - -

1868.

PRELIMINARY MEETING.

At a meeting of the Church and Congregation, September 15, 1867, it was voted, that the Two Hundredth Anniversary of the organization of this Church be celebrated with appropriate exercises; and that a Committee be appointed to make the necessary arrangements. Gen. Ely A. Elliot, Hon. Henry Taintor, Dr. D. H. Hubbard, George B. Hilliard, Esq., Capt. Dota L. Wright, and Rev. William E. Brooks, were appointed said Committee.

October 14th, Committee met at the residence of Gen. Ely A. Elliot, and selected the 13th of November, 1867, for the Bi-Centennial Anniversary.

Voted, That the Rev. Wm. E. Brooks be invited to prepare and deliver the Bi-Centennial Address.

Voted, That this Address be delivered at 10 and 1-2 o'clock, A. M., to be followed by a Collation served in the basement of the Church. The afternoon to be devoted to short speeches from invited guests.

Voted, That a Committee of twelve be appointed to arrange the tables, and direct the entertainment.

Voted, That Messrs. George E. Elliot, Alfred Davis, Ely Stannard, Jared Buell, Andrew J. Hurd, Samuel L. Stevens, Jr., Mrs. Henry A. Elliot, Mrs. Ely Stannard, Mrs. Jared Buell, Mrs. Leander Hull, Mrs. Silas Stannard, Mrs. Andrew J. Hurd, be said Committee.

D. H. HUBBARD, Secretary.

At an adjourned meeting held November 19, 1867, it was voted, that the very interesting Address by the Rev. Wm. E. Brooks, be published, and that a copy be requested for publication.

Voted, That the programme of the public exercises of said day, be also published with the Address.

ELY A. ELLIOT,
HENRY TAINTOR,
D. H. HUBBARD,   } *Committee.*
GEORGE B. HILLIARD,
DOTA L. WRIGHT,

D. H. HUBBARD, Secretary.

ANNIVERSARY.

The decorations of the Church for this festive occasion, were entrusted to a committee consisting of Mrs. Wm. E. Brooks, Mrs. Leander Hull, Miss Mary Leffingwell and Miss Roxanna Buell. They were assisted in the execution of their work, by a large number of the young ladies and gentlemen connected with the Church and Congregation, who brought willing hearts and ready hands to the task.

The building is a parallelogram, sixty-nine feet by forty, having a gallery on three sides, east, west and south. The north end being occupied by a recess for the pulpit and the platform.

The faces of these galleries were festooned with heavy ropes of the Ground Pine. Each loop encircling the name of one of the previous Pastors of this Church, commencing on the right hand as you enter, with WOODBRIDGE, and following round with PIERSON, ELIOT, HUNTINGTON, MANSFIELD, TALCOTT, WOOD, FOSTER, HINE, HUNTINGTON, 2d, to the opposite side, where it ended with MOORE. Brooks, the name of the present beloved Pastor, appeared in large letters on the front of the Pulpit. The letters which composed these names were formed of the shining, dark green leaves of the Mountain Laurel. This produced a very beautiful effect, as each name, encircled by its evergreen wreath, stood out clear and distinct on the white background. Mrs. Henry Taintor contributed two Harps wrought of Laurel, with minute flowers of Golden Immortelles for strings. These were placed on each side of the south gallery, devoted to singers. The unfading Laurel, a beautiful symbol, that the memory of the lives of the departed shall remain evergreen in the hearts of the people; although long ere this, all but two have gone to strike their Golden Harps where Flowers Immortal bloom.

The decorations over the Pulpit were designed by Miss Roxanna Buell, and consisted of an Arch on the front of the recess, reaching half way down the side. On the right hand of the speaker, the base rested on an oil painting of the Church edifice erected in Seventeen Hundred and Thirty-one.* On the speaker's left, at the base of the Arch, was a fine portrait of the Rev. Dr. Jared Elliot. Directly under the centre of the Arch, and following its curve, was a section of a few feet, the whole covered with white, and wreathed with a heavy border of the Ground Pine, interspersed with the shining red berries of the Bitter-sweet. On the outer Arch was inscribed in letters of Laurel, similar to those before mentioned, this motto:

"HE WHO PLANTED HAS SUSTAINED."

On the right hand side of the under section, was the date 1667, wrought in Autumn leaves. On the left, in leaves of Laurel, was the date 1867. Between them, and directly in the centre, were two hands, clasped. The one representing 1667, was composed of Autumn

---

*December 24, 1730.   *   *   *   It was also agreed by voat, that in case they build a new meeting house, it shall be set on the hill where the meeting house now standeth where it shall be judged most convenient. It was also agreed that sd meeting house should be 60 foots in length, 38 foots in breadth, and 22 foots between joynts, and a suitable turrit to be carryed out at one end suitable to hang ye Bell in.

leaves. The one representing 1867, of Laurel. The whole speaking plainly this sentiment:—1667 in the sere and yellow leaves of the past, reaches down Two Hundred Years, and with its withered hand, clasps the fresh vigorous hand of 1867, bringing this congratulatory message : Although bitter has been mingled with the sweet in past experiences, still, He who planted has sustained. Yea, and will sustain, until we exchange the Laurel of Time for the Tree of Life in Eternity.

On the left hand side of the platform below the Pulpit, was a pannel, taken from the Rev. Dr. Jared Elliot's house, on which was painted a view of the hill,* and of the second Church, erected in Seventeen Hundred. Seated on a rock in front of the house, is Dr. Elliott, and either he was a very large man, or the Church was very small, or the artist had some singular notions of perspective, as the Rev. gentleman's head is on a level with the eaves of the building. Hovering in the air is an American eagle, which the artist must have seen in a prophetic vision, so large is he painted. The ledges of rocks on the east bank of Indian River, are clearly defined and easily recognized. This painting

---

*Whereas the town, at a town meeting December 6th, 1698, had agreed to have an addition to the meeting house by gallaryes, the towns men, who were imployed there in, meeting with difficulties in their way, whether the town ware not better to buld a New meeting house then to make an Addition to the old by gallaries, this the town, haveing ben now called to gather to considar, they have now by thur voat agreed to buld a New meeting house, and they have agreed that the meeting house shall be five & thirty foots square, and to stand whare the old house now stands or whear convenient their unto."

At a town meeting in Killingworth, January 28, 1728, * * * * Also it was agreed by voat, that the meeting house shall be repaired as to the walling and covering, so as to secure it from being *Damnified* by the weather.

was executed by an artist from Boston, in the year 1710,—and is a curiosity.

On the right hand of the platform stood the old chair of Rector Pierson, kindly loaned for the occasion by Yale College, and occupied by Prof. D. C. Gilman, as its representative.

The occasion was one of the most heartfelt interest. The spirits of the men whose names we had before us, and whose lives and noble deeds we had assembled to commemorate, appeared to be with us. By some magnetic influence we seemed to be put in direct communication with the Spirit Land, and messages of Hope, and Love, and Cheer lifted our souls far above the ordinary level of existence. Great praise is due to the Rev. Wm. E. Brooks, for the able manner in which he performed his part as historian. Few could have so grasped the spirit of the lives and achievements of these departed worthies, and have brought it so eloquently before us. The hearts of the crowded audience were stirred with emotion, and smiles and tears held alternate sway.

ANNIVERSARY EXERCISES.

———— • ♦ • ————

The Exercises of the Bi-Centenial Celebration of the Clinton Congregational Church, were held in their house of worship, the Thirteenth of November, Eighteen Hundred and Sixty-eight. A most unusual and unseasonable storm of snow prevailed throughout the previous day. During the night, however, the storm ceased, and the morning of the Thirteenth rose clear and bright, with the thermometer nearly at zero, and a hard frozen crust of snow on the ground. Despite the unpropitious weather, the Church was filled to overflowing.

The Choir, under the direction of **Mr. Elias M. Dibbell,** opened the morning service with the old tune of "Denmark," "Before Jehovah's awful throne."

Invocation by Rev. Wm. E. Brooks.

Singing.—Hymn composed by Miss Wealtha Maria Hilliard.

TUNE—"AMERICA."

"Our fathers' God, to thee,
In this, our jubilee,
    To thee we sing:
Thy holy name we praise
In our most joyful lays,
For all thy wondrous ways,
    Great God, our King.

"Our kindred hearts here meet
And hold communion sweet
    Friend with his friend.
While from the courts above
Thy smiles, O God of love,
Our worship to approve,
    On us descend.

"Thy grace, O God, impart,
Unto each waiting heart
　　Before thee now.
Do thou our praises own,
And let thy power be shown,
While here before thy throne
　　We humbly bow.

" Help us to serve thee still,
Teach us to do thy will
　　In all our ways:
And thus, a light divine,
Reflected, Lord, from thine,
O'er all our lives shall shine
　　Through endless days."

Reading of the Scriptures and Prayer, by the Rev. James D. Moore. Psalm read, the 90th, commencing with " Oh ! Lord thou hast been our dwelling place in all generations."

HYMN.

God of our fathers, to thy throne
Our grateful songs we raise ;
Thou art our God,—and thou alone,—
Accept our humble praise.

Here thou wert once the pilgrim's guide ;
Thou gav'st them here a place,
Where freedom spreads its blessings wide,
O'er all their favored race.

Here, Lord, thy gospel's holy light
Is shed on all our hills;
And, like the rains and dews of night
Celestial grace distills.

Still teach us, Lord, thy name to fear
And still our guardian be ;
O, let our children's children here,
Forever worship thee.

HISTORICAL DISCOURSE.

————•••••————

INTRODUCTION.

In giving a Historical Sketch of this Church on this, its Two Hundredth Anniversary, I shall be forced to throw myself on your Christian charity and your kindly forbearance.

The few months which have elapsed since my settlement here, and the brief time allowed me to collect and arrange the materials from which a history might be written, must be my apology for whatever lack of detail there may be, and the passing by of most important and interesting facts. But what I have been able to accomplish in the time allotted me, and amid the pressure of other duties, I will now place before you.

It gives me great pleasure to acknowledge the assistance which I have received from the older members of the Church, in respect to the former pastors, and the events of by-gone days ; and my indebtedness to the Rev. J. D. Moore for the information I have obtained from the Historical Sketches which were published in " The Clinton Advertiser ;" to these persons, in a great measure, is due whatever of interest there may be in the present Discourse.

DISCOURSE.

" Lord, Thou hast been our dwelling place in all generations."— Ps. xc : 1.

The statement has somewhere been made, that the history of the world is but a history of God's Church : and so it may be said with especial truth, that the history of this town is to a great extent the history of this Church, and so closely are they united, that a brief notice of the former is essential to a clear and full knowledge of the latter.

The first name of this place was Hammonassett, so called after a tribe of Indians that lived upon these hills and roamed along these shores.

In 1663, at the October Session of the General Court that convened at Hartford, it was resolved, "that there should be a plantation formed at Hammonassett, and S. Willis, Mr. Wolcott, and Wm. Wadsworth, were appointed a committee for the ordering of the plantation at Hammonassett," who concluded on nine binding articles to be observed.

The 9th was, "That there shall be thirty families on the east side of Hammonassett River at the least."

The committee then entered twenty as planters. Soon after, ten of this number deserted the place ; and it was not till December, 1665, two years after the grant of the Assembly, that the required number of families had located themselves upon the "new plantation ;" and even then it was necessary to call the parsonage lot 29, and the minister's first lot 30.

The 7th article read thus : "They shall settle an able, orthodox, godly minister, free from scandal, with the advice of the major part of the magistrates of Connecticut." Thus we see that this Church was provided for at the very outset, and formed, if I may so speak, a part of the town, so that, as stated at the first, the one is inseparably linked to the other. And there can be no doubt that among the first buildings erected was the "Meeting House," small in size, but sufficiently large to accommodate the few, who were here to attend church,* till 1700, when the "new meeting house was built."†

---

* At a Town meting: November: 15th: 1703, the town have agreed, and Conclued by their voate to have a scoll houes bult: of sixteen foot square besides rome for the chimmie, and to be set on the meting houes hill whear judged most conveniant—allso the town have agreed: and voted that they wold have a skol: keept this year ackording to Law: and on halfe of the time to be keept in the winter and the other in the sumer. All so Atenry Crane Senior is voted and made Choyce of for a skoll master for the year insuing, for a leven shillings per weack.

All so town voted to take down the old meting hous and to improve it to buld a skool houes.

† Town meeting, Kenillworth, January the 18: 1704: * *
The town have agreed with Samuel Buell Senior to hew Draw and

The Rev. Mr. Moore, in his historical sketches, states that previous to the organization of the Church, a Mr. John Colton labored among the people ; but who he was, whence he came or whither he went, I know not, as I have been unable to learn anything more concerning him. It is quite evident, however, that they were wont to hold weekly service, for on the 28th of Sept., 1666, " the town bargained and agreed with Nathan Parmelee for forty shillings per year to beat the drum Sabbath days, for the calling of the people together, and to *maintain the drum at his expense ;*" and it is more than probable that this custom continued till a bell was procured, for on April 14th, 1668, " The town agreed with Samuel Gris-- wold to beat the drum Sabbath days for one year and to give him one pound and ten shillings,"* a novel and curious way of calling people to the worship of God.

The first two recorded votes for the support of the ministry were the following : " Feb. 7th, 1667. The town voted to free Mr. Woodbridge from paying any rate for two hundred Pounds estate, during his abode with us."

2d. The town voted to give him (Mr. Woodbridge,) " Fifty-five Pounds for the ensuing year, and parsonage land and his transportation and a house ; and further, it is left with the committee, if he will not come for the above said sum, to give him five Pounds more,"—exhibiting even at that early day,— Yankee shrewdness in trade making.

The plantation continued to be known as Hammonassett till not far from May, 1667, when it "was called Kenilworth, after a town in Warwickshire, England, from which, according to tradition, some of the settlers at first emigrated." The

---

frame timbar for a school houes of twenty one foots, in length, sixteen foot wide, the timbar to be soficent and Drawen to the place appointed by the town for the skoole hous to stand, this to be finished at or before the last of Aprill next, and for his satisfaction the town have agreed to give him the frame of the old meeting house, and thirty five shillings in Currant paye next year.

* In the Town Records is found the following :

" At a town meeting, December 6th, 1698.   *   *   *
the town have agreed that there shall be a new Drum bought for the town."

name was gradually changed from Kenilworth, being spelt sometimes Kenelworth, Kenellworth, "and in the State records, Kenelmeworth until the year 1707. In that year Sarjant John Crane was chosen Town 'Clark.' From that time the name in his hand writing is Killingworth, and has remained so ever since."

It was, as I have already stated, in February, 1667, that the town voted to secure the services of Mr. Woodbridge ; and in October, of the same year, the following petition was forwarded to the General Assembly, which convened at Hartford on the tenth of that month :

" May it please the Honored Court : Whereas the plenary enjoyment of all the sacred ordinances and institutions of Christ, and all possible communion with him therein, is that one thing that we should desire and seek after, and all tedious and unnecessary remissenesse in the prosecution of so sacred a designe, grandly culpable ; and forasmuch as the Honored General Court haue formerly in their wisdome established that no persons or inhabitants within this Colony imbody themselves in a Church without their favorable approbation ; we the inhabitants of the Town of Kenelmeworth, in obedience to so, not more just then, necessary a law, humbly craue and entreat their benigne aspect and approving allowance of so profitable and desirable a work as the gathering of ourselves into Church order, for the full and regular enjoyment of the aforesaid ordinances and institutions. As we therefore beseech your acceptance of us and incouragement to us in this proceeding, so we humbly implore the Eye of Almighty God to guide you in all your affaires.

JOHN WOODBRIDGE,
EDWARD GRISWOLD,
WILL HEAYDEN.

" In the name & with the consent of the rest."
" Oct. 11th, '67.

This petition was forwarded to the General Court which had assembled at Hartford the day previous, and was granted in the following words :

" This Court, upon the petition of the inhabitants of Kenilworth, doe hereby declare and give them theire approbation and encouragement to gather themselves into Church order according to the order of the Gospell."

The precise day on which the Church was organized, I have not been able to learn ; but as the petition was not signed till the 11th of October,.(O. S.,) which would be the 22d, (N. S.,) and as Dr. Field, in his History of Middlesex County, says that it was within a few weeks, it was probably not far from this time, if not on this very day of the month, that the Church was organized.

Two hundred years ago, then, it may be to a day, on this hill, and near the spot we now occupy, this Church was duly established, and John Woodbridge, a young man of twenty-three, was ordained and installed its first pastor, concerning whom, I learn from Dr. Sprague's Annals, (Vol. 1st, page 129, &c.,) that he was the grandson of the Rev. John Woodbridge, a distinguished Non-conforming minister, and that his grand-mother was the daughter of the Rev. Robert Parker, who by his writings is well known to have been a strong friend and advocate of non-conformity. His father, whose name was also John, was born at Stanton, Wiltshire, England, about the year 1613, and was sent to Oxford to be educated, but, when the oath of conformity was required of him he refused, and was therefore obliged to leave the University. He then pur-sued his studies privately. "The ceremonies of the Church being rigorously enforced," and being deeply imbued with the spirit of dissent, he came to this country in company with his uncle, Rev. Thomas Parker, in 1634. In 1641 he married the daughter of the Hon. Thomas Dudley, and was ordained and installed first pastor of the Church in Andover, Mass., where John Woodbridge, the first pastor of this Church was born, in 1644, and graduated at Harvard College, in 1664. During a portion of the next three years, he was doubtless devoting him-self to the study of Theology, and became first pastor of this Church in 1667. "At his settlement he had allotted to him eight acres of land as a home lot, located on Main street, rest-ing on South street, in compliance with a vote passed February 15th, 1664 :"

"'That the first minister that is called and settled amongst us shall *haue* the lott that lyes by the high way that goes down to the landing place."

Besides, I find that he was allowed to *take* up and hold land the same as any other citizen, as the grant made by the General Court in 1671, proves :—

"The Court grants Mr. John Woodbridge, of Kenilworth, 250 acres of land for a farm, provided he take it up where it may not prejudice any former grant to any plantation or perticuler person."

In March, 1669, the town voted to give him "£60 towards the building of him a dwelling." His salary at this time was £60 per year, and fifty loads of wood. He first lived near where Elias Wellman now lives, and afterwards on the corner now known as the Stanton place. For twelve years he was pastor of this Church, and then, for reasons unknown to me, and contrary to the wishes of his flock, he resigned, and the same year (1679) was installed pastor of the Church in Wethersfield, where he remained till his death, in 1690, being about forty-six years of age.

His son, John Woodbridge, married Jemima Eliot, daughter of the Rev. Joseph Eliot, of Guilford, and grand-daughter of the Apostle Eliot ; and it may be of interest to you to learn that the town of Woodbridge, near New Haven—formerly Amity—was so named in honor of Benjamin Woodbridge, the first, and for forty-three years the only, pastor of the Church in that place, who was the grand-son of the first pastor of this Church ; and that on this 15th day of November, 1867, they are celebrating the 125th Anniversary of that Church.

So much in respect to him whose name stands first on the list, both as member and pastor ; and his worthy descent, together with the results of his labors, prove that he was indeed one of "the most excellent clergymen of Connecticut."

The first private donation or gift to the Church for the support of the ministry, was made by William Kelsey, and that you may know in what form it was made, I will give his words, as found in the "Old Church Records :"—

"Know all men by these presents :—that I, William Kelsey, of Killingworth, being desireous to promote Religion and the maintainance thereof according to my Power, do freely give, to be paid yearly and forever after my decease, Twenty Shillings in current country pay, to the Church of Killingworth, for the use of the ministery that shall from time to time be there called, and for the ensurance thereof I do firmly bind over my Land in the Neckfield, purchased of John Meigs, Jnr., unto the Church of Killingworth, and do give full Power to him or them that are or from Time to time shall be, Deacons of the said Church, or in Case of their absence, to any two of the Brethren thereof to demand, recover or dispose of the money as aforesaid, and upon refusal to pay or in Case of Non-solvency, to seize upon the Land and to use and improve it as they see cause, for the aforesaid end.

In witness whereof I do hereunto set my hand this present June 6th, 1674.

WILLIAM KELCEY."

This land was " resigned up into the Church," in May, 1676, by his son, John Kelcey.

It was a sad misfortune for the Church to lose Mr. Woodbridge. After his departure, dissensions and divisions sprang up, and it was not till 1694, fifteen years after, that they succeeded in securing as their second pastor, Abraham Pierson, ' the son of the Rev. Abraham Pierson, who was minister successively at Southampton, L. I., Branford, Ct., and Newark, N. J.' He was born probably at Southampton—though Dr. Sprague says at Lynn, Mass.,—in 1646, being thus two years younger than Mr. Woodbridge, and graduated at Harvard College in 1668. " He began to preach in 1669, and received a unanimous call from the people of Woodbridge, N. J., to become their pastor. But the people of his father's congregation, desiring him for an assistant, at once made overtures to him to be ' helpful to his father, in the exercise of his gifts in the ministry, for the space of a year.' " In 1672 they extended to him a formal call to become his father's colleague, which he accepted. On the death of his father, in August, 1678, he became sole pastor, and his salary was fixed at £80 per year, "with a supply of fire wood, and freedom from taxation." He continued their pastor till 1692, when, on account of difference* of opinion in respect to church government, he was dismissed. He immediately disposed of his property in Newark, and came into this State, and became, as already stated, the second pastor of this Church, in 1694.

He very happily succeeded in reconciling the differences which existed in the Church, and soon gained both the confidence and love of his people. At this time there were efforts being made to establish a College in Connecticut, in which he took a great interest. In 1700 he was chosen as one of those ministers who were designated by public consent to act as Trustees "to found, erect and govern a College." At a session of the General Colonial Assembly at New Haven, in October, 1701, a petition was presented to that body, signed by many ministers and others, which stated,—

"That from a sincere regard to and zeal for upholding the Protestant religion, by a succession of learned and orthodox men, they had proposed that a Collegiate School should be erected in this Colony, wherein youth should be instructed in all parts of learning to qualify them for public employments in Church and Civil State; and that they had nominated ten ministers to be trustees, partners or undertakers for founding, endowing or ordering the said School, and thereupon desired that full liberty and privilege might be granted to the said undertakers for that end."

On the 9th of the same month, the Assembly granted the desired charter; and at a meeting of the trustees on the 7th of November, 1701, Mr. Pierson was chosen to take charge of the College "in its instruction and government, with the title of Rector." Their choice was regarded as a happy one, as Mr. Pierson was both a fine scholar and took a deep interest in the cause of education. He had even then prepared a work on Natural Philosophy, which he introduced in the College, and which continued as a manual in that department for many years. The College building was established here in what was then Killingworth, near the edge of the Green, and a little south and east from the barn which stands on the Stanton Place, some of the beams of which are still to be seen in the "Stanton House." The building has been torn down within the memory of some of the older members of this congregation; so that the statement made by Dr. Sprague, that Mr. Pierson heard the recitations in his own house, is in part an error.

Not only did the Church prosper under his ministry, but the cause of education received an impulse which continues to be felt. It was during his pastorate that the old church building was torn down, and the second one was erected, (1700,) for which a bell—one of the first in Connecticut—was procured in 1703 ; in respect to which the following action of the town may be of interest :—

"At a meeting of the town held August 20th, 1703, * * * * it was offered unto the town, by several of the neighbors which had by subscription purchased a Bell in order to be *hung up in the meting houes*, whether they would accept of said Bell and hang it at the town charge, which was consented unto and voted."*

The following action of the town, on the 14th of December, 1695, shows how closely at that time the town and church were united :—

"The town being met together to consider of something to be done for the encouragement of Mr. Abraham Pierson, our present minister in his settlement with us—Do give the said Mr. Pierson the Town House and Orchard . . . upon the condition hereinafter named, that is to say, that the said Mr. Pierson shall plant an orchard of an hundred apple trees upon the parsonage land, where the town shall judge most convenient, and the said trees to manure and secure."—(" *Town Records.*")

But while the interests of both the Church and the College were in a most flourishing condition, the people of Saybrook felt anxious that the College should be removed to their town, which, as it would deprive them of a much loved pastor, the people of Killingworth bitterly opposed. Nay, more, they were unwilling that he should continue its Rector. At a town

---

* At a town meetin in Killingworth, December ye 29th, 1724.
* * * * *

"It was also voated that the town will be at the cost of haveing the bell belonging to the meeting house in Killingworth, new cast, or run with the adition of fifty pounds of Copper and one quarter so much puter, and that they will Imploy Mr. Liscome of Saybrook to Do the sd work, upon condition sd Liscome will do sd work for twelve pounds, if he will efect the same and that he will Demand nothing for his Labor if he fails in the well performanc of sd work." * * * *

Also ye meeting was adjourned untel ye 11th Day of this Instant november at sun *two Hours high at night.*

meeting held November 7th, 1706, he sent to them a request, in behalf of the trustees, that they would allow the College to remain in Killingworth, under his care. Even this they were unwilling to grant. It was while matters were in this disturbed state—his flock calling in one direction and the interests of education in another—that he sickened and died, falling asleep on the 5th of March, 1707, at the age of sixty-one.

His grave is in the north-western part of the cemetery, surrounded by the remains of those he loved, and may the day be not far distant, when a monument more worthy of his memory and record, shall mark the place where lived and labored Abraham Pierson, the second pastor of this Church, and first President of Yale College.*

---

* Knowing that all lovers of Yale College feel a deep interest in whatever pertains to its early history, has prompted to a careful searching of the early Town Records, wherein the following letters and votes have been found recorded :—

" To the Inhabitants of Killingworth :

Sirs,—Whareas I perceive that there is a misapprehention of my Answer at New Haven to the Reverend trustees of the Collegiate School, which was latly published, in part among you, I do declare as followith, viz, that in their motion to me there ware two things ; 1 : their Desire that I should take the care and conduct of the said school. 2, that I should remove with the school to the place by them appointed for it. to the 1st of these I Answered as you have heard ; the true meaning whereof was, that I Durst not Deny a Divine call to attend that work so far as was consistent with my ministerial work among you : and accordingly I have endeavoured to practise ever since. To the 2nd of them, not Discarning a present call thereunto ; after much perswasion and pressing to it, my Answer was to act therein as god should open my way : in which opening of my way, I ever included, your consent to my removal and never obliged myself to Remov without it, and by your consent I mean your General and Joyant consent, and not mearly a major part of you consenting ; that as through Divine favour I have lived among you in peace, now about a : 11 : years, so if I be removed from you, which is not at all of my seeking, I may leave you in peace, and have hope that the god of peace will be with you, and as a testimony of your general and joynt consent to my Removal, (if I do remove,) I expect your ingagement by sufficient sureties to Reimburse and according to a greement, without which I shall not part with the house, and with out this

In regard to his person Dr. Field thus speaks: "He was above a middling stature, was fleshy and well favored. As a Christian he was charitable and pious; in preaching he excelled, and by his character and talents was excellently qualified for the station to which he was advanced." Pres. Clapp says: "He was a hard student, a good scholar, a great divine, and a wise, steady and judicious man in all his conduct.

---

ingagement I shall not think I have a sufficient expression of your consent to my removal.

ABRAHAM PIERSON.

September 21: 1705."

To this letter the town made reply that, "We do declare that it is our opinion that it is not, or like to be consistent with your ministerial work amongst us to attend sd school as heitherto." They also made reply to his request, in case of their consenting to his removal, that they should reimburse him for his house, "that we shall not endeavor to act in that matter any firther than we have allready Don.

This voted in town meting November 25th 1705."

" At the above meeting (November 7th, 1706) it was proposed to the town by the Desire of Mr. Pierson in the behalf of the trustees, for the town's allowance for the Collegiate Scool to be & remain here under the care & conduct of the Reverend Mr. Pierson : the town have Declared by their vote that they are not willing to allowe that the School be keept hear as it has been."

At a town Meting in Kenillworth, December the 24th, 1706.

* * * *

Also the town Did make Choyce of Decon Griswold, Robert Lane, Sarjt John Shether, Sarjt Sam. Stevens, and Sarjt John Crane, as a Comity to consider of, and draw up sum terms or proposalls for the town to consider of with Respect to the allowance of the Collegiate School Being here under the care and conduct of Mr. Pierson, and to make return thear of to the next town meting."

What action would have been taken is uncertain. Mr. Pierson dying in March after, put a stop to all further proceedings. There can be no doubt that Mr. Pierson exerted a great influence in arousing the people of this town to a higher regard to the demands of Education. This is indicated by the fact that in 1696, two years after his settlement, " the town concluded by their voat to hire mr. Brown to keep skoul for one quarter of a year, and for his pains there in to give him nine pounds : the one half of it to be paid by the skollers and the other halfe by the town," this being the first school of which we have any record, and the first school house was built in 1703.

About fifty-four were gathered in during his ministry of about thirteen years ; a number, without doubt, equal to the whole membership at his coming.

The third pastor was the Rev. Jared Eliot, D.D. and M. D., a grandson of the Apostle Eliot and son of the Rev. Joseph Eliot, of Guilford, where he was born on the 7th of Nov., 1685. He graduated at Yale College in 1706, under President Pierson, by whom he was recommended to this Church as one in every respect worthy to become his successor and their pastor. Accordingly, in June following Mr. Pierson's death, a call was extended to Mr. Eliot ; but doubting his ability to fulfill so great a trust, he was not ordained till Oct. 26th, 1709.* The following will give you a glimpse of the times in which he lived :

"At a Town Meeting held in Killingworth Nov. 25th, 1608 : The Town do agree to give to Mr. Jared Eliot when he, the said Jared Eliot, shall marry, or have a family, sixty loads of good fire wood a year."

---

* "At a Town Meeting held in Killingworth, September ye 26 : 1709, the Town did by their vote conclude to Indever that Mr. Jared Eliot be settled a monst us in office, (or ordayed) on ye Last Wednesday of october next insueing.

"Also the Town do agree that the Charge of the Ordaination of Mr. Eliot shall be boren or paid by a Rate Levied upon the Estates of ye subscribers to the Covenant in the Town, allwaye provided yt any other person is not bared from doing what they shall see cause. * *

"Also that there shall be a foundation Laied for the Galleries on ye South Side in the Meeting House before the ordination of Mr. Eliot.

"At a Town Meeting, March ye 7th, 1712, The town have agreed to finish ye for part of the Gallery in the meeting house, both stairs seats & banesters.

"Also at the same meeting the town granted liberty to those persons that will appear to make or build the foundation of the galery on ye East & West Sides of ye meeting house and put up ye banesters, provided they doe it upon their own cost and charg : not claiming perticuler right in the account thereof : The Town made choice of Leftt : Samuel Buel, Sargtt Josiah Stevens & Gersiam Palmer as a Comete to cary on the work of finishing fore gallery in the meeting house.

"March ye 12th 1712 * * .* * The Comite for finishing the frunt galery are appaynted to manag the other part of building & finishing sd Galiryes."

Two inferences readily suggest themselves. Either the people were anxious that he should fulfill the Scriptures by becoming the husband of one wife, or they thought he spent too much of his time in Guilford in the winning and enchanting society of Miss Elizabeth Smithson, to whom he was married Oct 26th, 1710. That the amount of wood first promised was insufficient is shown by the fact that on the 17th of Nov., 1741—

"£40 were appropriated to procure Mr. Eliot 80 loads of wood, at ten shillings per load, for the year ensuing; and, if any person neglect his just proportion of wood to Mr. Eliot, as aforesaid, at or by ye first day of Jan. next coming, they shall pay their proportion to ye Minister's Collector to procure wood for Mr. Eliot." There was also, on the 14th of Dec. of the same year, a vote of "£120 to pay ye Rev. Mr. Eliot's Salary for ye year past, to be paid in Bills of publick credit, or in provision, at the Current market price, exclusive of ye use of parsonage and his wood."

It is stated that his early progress in letters was not rapid, but that what he once gained he never lost. The further he advanced in knowledge the stronger his mind became, and increased also in quickness of apprehension, and, at length, he acquired a greatness and excellence rarely surpassed in this country.

Rev. Thomas Ruggles, who preached his funeral sermon, said: "His person was well proportioned. The dignity, and gravity, and openness of his countenance were plain indications of the penetration of his mind, and the agreeable turn of his conversation. He was favored with an excellent bodily constitution. Idleness was his abhorrence, and every moment of time was filled with action by him. Perhaps no man slept so little in his day and did so much in so great a variety. His endowments of mind were no less superior than his bodily vigor. A sound mind in a sound body was what he was blest with; and his great soul shined like the sun in the firmament with radiant luster. Always active, always bright and pleasant. He had a mind peculiarly adapted for conversation and happily accommodated to the pleasures of social life. Nothing affected, nothing assumed. It was all nature. Divinity he made his chief study. He understood what he preached to others in a very large compass of knowledge, in the theory of Theology. He was truly a good preacher in a proper sense. Though he never studied to shine in rhetoric, and the enticing words of men's wisdom, yet his discourses were always instructive and entertaining. Differences as to religious principles, were no obstruction to the hearty practice of the great law of love—true benevolence and true goodness to man—to every man. He abhorred narrowness and the mean contractedness of party spirit. As he claimed the right to think and act for himself, so was he more than free to accord the same privilege to others. As a physician, he was quick to determine the nature of the disease, and to apply the proper remedy. He was especially successful in his treatment of that dread disease—dropsy. His practice becoming extensive, he was called many miles from home ; and, that he might not lose time, he acquired the habit of reading on horseback. Here, also, he thought out many of his sermons." He would, while traveling along, become so absorbed in thought, as to be entirely oblivious to what was taking place around him ; and his horse, taking advantage of this, was wont to stop and graze by the roadside, or turning into the field would pursue his own course, till Mr. Eliot, arousing up, would find himself—not as he hoped—many miles nearer his journey's end, but facing a haystack.* He possessed the power of losing himself in his subject.

" Although so actively engaged, he was seldom absent from his charge on the Sabbath ; and for more than forty years of the latter part of his life, he never missed of preaching some part of every Sabbath, either at home or abroad."

" He had a scientific turn of mind, and for discovering the fact that black sand might be wrought into iron, he received a

---

* The following incident will illustrate another phase of his character : One Sabbath morning just before starting for Church, he discovered a rent in his long black silk stocking, which he repaired, not by calling in the aid of Mrs. Eliot, but by applying with his pen, ink to the exposed part, and with the rent thus concealed, he gave himself to the duties of the Sabbath.

gold medal from the society instituted in London for the Encouragement of Arts, Manufactures and Commerce,—an honor seldom conferred on a citizen of this country. He was fond of society ; and by a pleasant and sociable temper connected with his talents, he was eminently qualified to secure and entertain friends. His acquaintances and correspondents were numerous, among whom were Dr. Franklin and Bishop Berkley. He was liberal. As a physician he did much without charge. But while he scattered, he increased ; and being a man of fine business talent, he acquired a large amount of land which proved a source of wealth to a large family."

As might be supposed, the Church was greatly prospered, as is clearly shown by the fact that during his ministry of fifty-six years, some five hundred and twenty-seven were gathered in.

For the last thirty-two years of his life he was a member of the Corporation of Yale College.

His home was just across the street in front of the Church, and stood where the cottage occupied by the widow Dee now stands,—before which Nature has reared up a beautiful and graceful Elm—a living monument, and fit emblem of him, who, while he lived, was a joy to the sorrowing, a health-giver to the sick, a promoter of the sciences, a true lover of his country, a devoted follower of Christ, and a rich and lasting blessing to this Church.

He died April 22d, 1763, aged 77 years and 5 months.

The fourth pastor was the Rev. Eliphalet Huntington, who was born in Lebanon, Conn., in 1737, graduated at Yale College in 1759, and was licensed by the Hartford South Association, Oct., 1761.

On the 22d of May, 1763, just one month after the death of Dr. Eliot, he preached for the first time to this people, being then in his twenty-sixth year. At a meeting of the Church, held on the 20th of December of the same year, it was voted, "That Mr. Eliphalet Huntington be desired to accept the united call of the First Society of Killingworth, and also to take the pastoral charge of this Church." He accepted, and was ordained and installed January 11th, 1764.

There were two votes passed some two weeks after Mr. Huntington first preached here, which may be of interest :

" 1st. Voted that ye Committee are Desired to engage Mr. Hunting-ton for a longer term of time to supply ye pulpit.

2d. Voted that ye Society are desireous of having the Funeral Sermon of ye Dr. Eliot printed and that ye Society are desired to apply to Revd Mr. Ruggles for a copy of the same, to be done at ye expense of ye Society."

At a meeting held Jan. 17th, 1764, it was voted

" That the Society's Committee take care and see that the Rev. Mr. Huntington be supplied with necessary fire wood for the current year, at the expense of the Society.

He was voted £200 for settlement, to be paid in annual payments of £50. His salary was;

1st. £40 per year, for four years, after which it should be £50.

2d. The use of parsonage land, calculated to be worth a yearly rent of £25.

4th. The Society likewise vote and grant for the further encourage-ment & support of sd Mr. Huntington necessary fire wood, during his continu in sd work, as aforesaid, according as he may stand in need of for his own use, not exceeding sixty cart loads annually, to be provided sumtime in the month of November annually."

This was recorded Jan. 25, 1764. He was married April 24th, 1766, being then about twenty-nine years of age, to Miss Sarah Eliot, grand-daughter of Rev. Dr. Eliot, who was not at that time quite fifteen,—almost if not quite justifying a remark she is said to have made, that " Mr. Huntington was old enough to be her father." He died of small-pox, Feb. 8, 1777, having been pastor of this Church a little more than thirteen years.

In person he was large and portly, very pleasant and agree-able in his intercourse with all ; and won a place in the hearts of his people. " He was strongly attached to the doctrines of Grace,—a warm, zealous and eloquent preacher." He preached at the meeting of the General Association, which met in Nor-wich in 1775, from which I infer that he was regarded as " one of Connecticut's most able ministers." There were above sixty added to the Church during his pastorate. He lived in the house now occupied by Gen. E. A. Elliot.

Achillies Mansfield was the fifth pastor. He was born at New Haven in 1751. Graduated at Yale College in 1770. Licensed by the New Haven East Association in 1775. Began to preach for this people the 17th of August, 1777, being then twenty-six years of age. On the 17th of December, 1778, a call was given him to become pastor, which he accepted, and was ordained and installed January 6th, 1779. It was voted :

" 1st. That there be given to Mr. Achillies Mansfield, on condition of his settling amongst us in the work of the Gospel Ministry, the sum of 600 ounces of silver, or in bills of credit to the value thereof, to be improved by him at his discretion, towards providing himself with a convenient tenement for his accommodation among us, to be collected & paid in four equal payments annually.

" 2d. That there be granted unto Mr. Mansfield as a yearly salary, for the four years first after his being regularly inducted into the work of the Gospel Ministry among us, the sum of 135 ounces of Silver or in Bills of Credit to the value thereof, to be paid Mr. Mansfield on the first day of January, annually, until the term of four years be completed ; and after the expiration of four years coming, this Society do hereby grant to Mr. Mansfield the sum of 180 ounces of Silver annually, during his continuance in the office of the Gospel Ministry among us ; & to be computed and paid to him in Wheat at the rate of 5 shillings per bushel; or Rye at three shillings per bushel ; or Indian Corn at 2 shillings per bushel ; or in Pork at four pence per pound ; or in Beef at two pence per pound ; or in other articles in like proportion ; or in Bills of Credit to the value thereof."

He was also allowed the use of the Parsonage or Society lands, and the sixty cart loads of good wood annually.

On March the 10th, 1779, he married the widow of the Rev. Eliphalet Huntington, by whom he had three children—Elizabeth, who married Dr. Olcott ; Nathan, who graduated at Yale College in 1803, studied medicine, and died in 1813 ; and Susan, who married the Rev. Joshua Huntington, of Boston.

A gentlemen, who was a member of his congregation and knew him well, has kindly furnished me the following :

" The Rev. Achillies Mansfield was of medium height, of good form, and had a very pleasant countenance. He was courteous and affable in his manners, and upon all occasions gave good evidence of a sincere desire to promote the interest of his Master's Kingdom. His voice was good, being clear and full. In the delivery of his sermons he was lively and interesting and very punctual in the performance of all his duties as pastor. In extempore speaking, at funerals and like occasions, he had few equals; for, possessing a tender and sympathetic heart, he felt keenly for those in affliction, and so, prompted by his own kindly nature, he was in an especial degree fitted to soothe and console the sorrowing.

It was during his ministry that evening meetings were established, being held in the Old Stone School House which then stood a little east of the Church. He conducted the meetings thus: After the preliminary exercises, such as prayer and singing, he would read the chapter selected for the occasion and then explain it verse by verse, remaining seated. All who attended these exercises well remember, how, after reading a verse or two, he would stop, sit back, raise his spectacles, and then explain and enforce the truths of the passage. Few, if any, surpassed him in like efforts; and the meetings were well attended and appreciated."

He was six years a member of the Corporation of Yale College, being so at his death. He was faithful and attentive in the discharge of his duties to that Institution, and was ever desirous of promoting its interests. He was very popular with his associates, and his death was regarded as a severe loss to them and the flock which he loved.

Dr. Field says: "He was a man distinguished for mild and pleasant manners, for uniformity and sweetness of disposition, and for the patient endurance of affliction." Here for thirty-seven years he preached to this people, and for the whole time, lacking two years, their pastor,—and he had the joy of welcoming one hundred and eighty-two to the Sacramental Feast. On the Sabbath preceding his death he preached from the text, "His rest shall be glorious." He lived in the house now occupied by Esquire Taintor, where he died July 22d, 1814, aged sixty-three.

It was during his ministry that Dr. Benjamin Gale, who married a daughter of the Rev. Dr. Eliot, died. I refer to him because, in one sense, he stands connected with the history of this Church, and because I desire to call your attention to the fact that even then there were those in this place that were looking for the speedy destruction of the present order of things. He built the stone house, which, with some improvements, is now known as "The Clinton House." It is said that he had its walls made thick and strong, so that it might stand till he should rise from the dead, so that he could have a home to go to, and one that should look natural. Some state that he set out the cedar which stands in front of it, but others say,—which is far more probable,—that it was there at the first settlement of the town, and is therefore one of the oldest, if not *the oldest* tree in this section of the country,—a living link connecting us to "the long, long ago." He was buried according to his request, with his feet towards his home, facing the west, so that, as he said, the first thing he should behold on coming forth from the grave, would be his old Homestead. Well, the house still stands, and as far as I can judge, is likely to for years,—perhaps for centuries yet to come ; in front of it the cedar still sways, looking as if weary with its long vigil ; and for your comfort, who desire to so think, his dying wish may yet be gratified ; at any rate, those of you who may wish to visit his grave, will find the following, in letters almost effaced by the finger prints of time :

"In memory of Dr. Benjamin Gale, who, after a life of usefulness in his profession, and a laborious study of the prophecies, fell asleep May the 6th, A. D. 1790, Æt. 75, fully expecting to rise again under the Messiah and to reign with Him on Earth. 'I know that my Redeemer liveth, and that He shall stand at the latter day upon the Earth, and mine eyes shall behold Him and not another.'"

Rev. Hart Talcott was the sixth pastor. He was born at Bolton, Conn., graduated with honor at Dartmouth College in 1812, studied theology at Andover, where, at the end of three years, he graduated with the highest honors of his class, and was licensed by the Tolland Association, June 4th, 1816. He was invited to preach in the 1st Congregational Church of New Haven, and but for his lack of voice would have received, it is said, their unanimous invitation to settle as their pastor.

In 1817 he received and accepted a call to become pastor of this Church, and was ordained and installed the 11th of June of the same year. At his own request he was dismissed June 14th, 1824.

During the first part of his ministry here he lived on the place now owned by Mr. Horace Barker, in an old house which has since been removed. In 1823 the Parsonage was erected, and he became its first occupant. After leaving here he was settled in Warren of this State, where he died in March, 1836, greatly beloved and lamented. "As a writer," says one that knew him well, "he was preëminent. His style was chaste, and his reasoning cogent. His sermons when ready for the pulpit were also ready for an Edinburgh Review. Had he possessed sufficient vocal powers, he could have commanded, as those well qualified to judge declare, some of the best locations in our State or land. He was a man of excellent social qualities,—modest, unassuming, and only anxious to spend and be spent in his Master's service."

During his pastorate of six and one-half years, eighteen were gathered into the Church.

After his dismission, a serious division arose in the Church in regard to employing the Rev. Peter Crocker, against whom charges of immorality were circulated. So bitter became the feeling, that a portion of the Church refused to listen to him, and, having withdrawn, worshiped by themselves. There being dissatisfaction also with the Consociation on account of the course the members pursued, formal votes of secession from the Consociation were passed at Church meetings held on May the 5th and June the 28th, 1830, which I will quote, in order to show how squarely they took their stand on pure Congregational grounds :

"At a regular meeting of the 1st Church in Killingworth, held at the meeting house, this, the 28th day of June, 1830, it was voted, that this Church do not consider themselves in any way as a Consociated Church, and do stand on the same foundation and footing as it respects Consociation, as the first Church of Christ in Guilford, which has never been Consociated, and that the Consociation have no right, nor any of their ministers, to intermeddle with the right of this Church to appoint its own officers, examine and receive members into the Church, or any other of the concerns of this Church, unless requested by the Church."

On this new basis the Church were again united, and on the 5th of Sept., 1831, at a regular meeting of the Church, it was unanimously voted :

"That we concur with the 1st Ecclesiastical Society of Killingworth in giving the Rev. Luke Wood a call to settle with us in the work of the Gospel Ministry, and also to take pastoral charge of this Church."

And at a Church Meeting held on the 26th of the same month, the following action was taken, viz :—

"Whereas, this Church and the 1st Ecclesiastical Society in Killingworth have given to the Rev. Luke Wood a call to settle with them in the work of the Gospel Ministry, and he having accepted the call, voted, That we sincerely invite those that once professed to belong to this Church, and are still in good standing, to come together with us upon the same foundation and standing, as it respects Consociation, as the 1st Church in Guilford ; and also all those that made a public profession of their faith, and partook of the Sacrament at the Union Prayer Meeting, held at the Meeting House in this place in the summer of 1830. And we also wish them to unite with us in the Installation and settlement of the Rev. Luke Wood over the Church and Society in the work of the Gospel Ministry."

This was acceded to, and Mr. Wood was installed the 13th of October, 1831.

I have given somewhat in full the action of the Church for two reasons : First, that the real condition of affairs in the Church might be seen ; and second, that it might be apparent to all how difficult and peculiar was the position of Mr. Wood. Great tact and skill were necessary to unite in one harmonious whole, the then so lately separate and discordant elements. That he was successful two facts will prove : First, the Church remained united ; and second, during his pastorate of two and one-half years, thirty-one were added to the Church, and all but two on profession of faith. He was dismissed March, 1834.

Rev. Mr. Wood was born at Somers, Conn., in 1777 ; graduated at Dartmouth College in 1803 ; took his second degree in course, and also at Yale ; studied Theology with Dr. Emmons ; was licensed by Hartford North Association, and ordained pastor of the First Congregational Church of Waterbury, Conn., November 30th, 1808, where he continued till dismissed on account of severe sickness in 1817. Upon his recovery, he engaged in Missionary labors in other states, organizing, during the time, the Congregational Church in Agawam, Mass. ; after this he came to Killingworth. From here he went to Queechy, Vt. ; thence he became pastor of the Church in West Hartland, from which he was dismissed in 1842. Being then far advanced in life, he returned to Somers, his birth place, where he spent the remaining years of his life doing good, teaching a Bible class and occasionally preaching. The Rev. Mr. Wood died August 22d, 1851, aged 74.

In the Congregational Journal of February 4th, 1852, it is stated that—

"His (Mr. Wood's) opinion; on the subject of the education of the female sex more particularly, were formed on a high standard of female character. On this point his views were greatly in advance of the prevailing sentiment during the early years of his ministry; yet with the judicious and reflecting class of parents they had great weight; and not a few among the more highly educated women of Connecticut owe, in part, their superior advantages to the influence of his views upon others."

In the Congregational Quarterly of 1859, may be found the following :

"Mr. Wood was eminently successful as a pastor, and did much to heal the wounds in Christ's Church, and to build up her waste places. His preaching was direct and practical in a good sense."

The eighth pastor was Lewis Foster, who was born at Hartland, Conn., in 1806 ; graduated at Yale College in 1831 ; studied at New Haven Theological Seminary ; was licensed by New Haven West Association in 1834, and was ordained and installed pastor of this Church, December 3d, 1834, and died October 27th, 1839, after a brief ministry of four years and ten months, during which eighty-one were gathered into the Church.

Mr. Foster was a little above the medium height, and a little inclined to stoop. As a preacher he was earnest, argumentative and *spiritual*, the great, all absorbing desire of his life being to build up and advance the cause of Christ. He loved his flock deeply, his wife often hearing him in the quiet hours of the night, when he thought those around him wrapt in sleep, pleading with God for an outpouring of His Spirit upon the Church and people. It was during his ministry here, that the present Church edifice was erected, he preaching the dedication sermon from the text, "Thy way, O God, is in the Sanctuary."

His labors were eminently blessed, and having lived the same number of years that his Savior did, God called him from the scenes of earth, to the brighter and more radiant glories of heaven. He too sleeps in yonder yard, and at the head of his grave is a marble slab, erected by the members of his flock, as a slight token of the love they bore him ; a love which, to-day, after the lapse of more than twenty-eight years, is warm and glowing.

One, who was a member of his flock and prized him highly, says : "His ministry was brief but very successful. He won the affection of his people by his ardent devotion to his work, and his earnest and successful labors in the vineyard of his master, as well as by his genial and kindly disposition. The record shows a larger accession to the membership of the Church during his ministry, than for the same length of time in its previous history."

A friend relates the following incident illustrative of the predominant trait of his character. The people had assembled to erect the frame work of this building ; an unsuccessful attempt was made to raise a portion of it, when he stepped forward, and, amid the silent group, offered an earnest invocation for the blessing of Almighty God upon their efforts to rear, for His worship and glory, this house of prayer. Quietly and rapidly every timber was then placed in position, without accident or delay.

He was exceedingly sensitive. At one time he imagined that the people were dissatisfied with him, which lead him to indicate his purpose of leaving his field of labor ; but the spontaneous protest of his people convinced him, that he had been mistaken, and thereupon he remarked to one of the brethren, who assured him of the affectionate regard of his flock, that he was ready to live, labor and die among them,—which he did.
One, that had ample opportunity for observation, says, " That the time usually occupied by young ministers in rehearsing their sermons, previous to entering upon the labors of the pulpit, was uniformily spent by him, pleading with God for His blessing to rest upon his efforts." The prosperity of Zion was the great burden of his life. His death was deeply lamented by his charge, who still treasure his memory so fragrant with all that is precious and lovely in a devoted, humble Christain character."—Truly, " the memory of the just is blessed."

Orlo D. Hine, was the ninth pastor. He was born in New Milford, Conn. ; graduated at Yale College in 1837 ; licensed by New Haven West Association in 1840 ; was ordained and installed pastor of this Church, April 14th, 1841, and, at his own request, was dismissed October 25th, 1842. He was the first pastor of this Church after the town of Killingworth was divided, and the name of Clinton had been given to this portion, which was done at the May Session of the General Assembly in 1838. During his pastorate, twenty-one united with the Church. He is now, and for the last eleven years has been, pastor of the Church in Lebanon, of this State.

Enoch S. Huntington, was the tenth pastor, who was born in Ashford, Conn., September 30th, 1804 ; graduated at Amherst College, and studied Theology at Lane Seminary, Ohio. He spent the first of his ministerial life in the West, preaching for several years in Groveland, Tazwell Co., Ill. After a few years, his health failing him he was forced to come East. It was while at home, that he was recommended to this Church by Dr. Biles ; both he and the people being mutually pleased, he accepted a call to become their pastor, and was installed May 24th, 1843, and was, at his own oft expressed desire, dismissed March 26th, 1850. Sixty-eight united with the Church while he was its pastor. After leaving here he preached, as stated supply, to several Churches, and died in Danbury, Conn., April 7th, 1862.

Mr. Huntington, soon after his settlement here, was blest with one of the most extensive revivals ever enjoyed by this people. He entered into the work with his whole heart, laboring early and late for the salvation of those out of Christ.

His health,—none of the best at any time,—gradually failed him ; and being of a strong " nervo-billious temperament," aggravated by his labors in the West, he suffered, at times, intensely from melancholy, which unfitted him for mental or corporeal exercise. He would, when thus oppressed, seek retirement, being entirely incapacitated for visiting his flock, or making any suitable preparation for the Sabbath. Sermons, written with the greatest care, seemed, at such times, worthless, and he would have destroyed many of his best productions, had not his wife, having persuaded him to allow her to examine them, put them away for safe keeping, till his despondency should be in a measure past. Often the whole service of the Sabbath was a terrible trial to him, feeling that his prayers were soulless, his preaching of no power, and he would go home and weep over what seemed to him his weak and inefficient efforts; during such seasons, he thought himself unfit to preach, and would determine, without delay, to have a council called for his dismission.

By the judicious management of his wife, who would urge him to take carriage exercise, his life was prolonged many years. The following incident will illustrate the nervous excitability of the man: The neighboring ministers, on a certain occasion, were to meet at his house and take dinner with him. The butcher failed to appear with the desired beef, and, having sought in vain for a substitute, he came home all excitement, exclaiming, "Wife, wife! what shall be done? ten or a dozen brother ministers to take dinner with us, and we have nothing to give them!" "Do not worry, Mr. Huntington, you take care of the ministers, and I will attend to the table." "But wife, we *must* have something to eat, and I can find neither flesh, fish nor fowl." "Have faith, have faith, Mr. Huntington; God will provide; just leave it with Him." "Yes, but what will He provide, codfish and potatoes? You are all faith, but I think it about time for works. Only look,—in one half hour, and my brethren will be here, and we have nothing for dinner." "True, but I assure you, that there shall be enough and well cooked." While this debate was going on, a knock was heard, and upon going to the door, Mrs. H. found one of their parishioners, who said: "We have been killing some nice roasters, and, thinking that our pastor might like one, have brought this, which, I hope, may be acceptable." It is needless to say, that Mr. Huntington felt rebuked; and with tears he acknowledged his lack of faith in the loving and providing care of God.

The eleventh pastor was James D. Moore, who began his ministry the tenth day of March, 1850, and ended his labors as pastor on Sunday, the 4th day of March, 1866—a ministry of just sixteen years. As one result of his labors, one hundred and twenty-three were gathered into the Church; and if those who united on the first Sabbath in May, after his departure, be added, it will increase the number to one hundred and seventy-six. He is now pastor of the Congregational Church in Plainfield, Conn.

Of him, or his, or his works, I need not speak. His pleasant face, his kindly beaming eye, his cordial greeting, his loving heart,—these are household treasures—present to you all. His deep and sincere sympathy especially endearing him to the afflicted. As a citizen, he was an ardent lover of his adopted country ; as a man, he was honored and respected ; as a pastor, he possessed the confidence of his flock, as one who really desired to do them good ; and as a friend, he was loved. He especially desired that his people might not only be Christians, but intelligent ones.

Your present pastor was ordained and installed, May 23d, 1867.

In looking back over the history of this Church, we find that there have been, including the present, *four* " Meeting Houses." The first which was built at the first settlement, and lasted till the year 1700. The second was then built, for which a bell was procured in 1703 ; and in which galleries were made in 1709. In 1731, the third was erected, upon which a new steeple was raised in 1809, as is shown by the following entry by Mr. Mansfield :

" 1809, June 1st. The new steeple was raised to the meeting house. The meeting house was then about seventy-eight years old."

It faced the West, the principal entrance being on the South. It had galleries, high pulpit on the side—under which was the Deacons' seat,—and its "pews" were high and square. In the foundation wall of this building, near the South-east corner, may be seen the stone step, which was at the South or principal entrance, worn smooth by the countless steps of our fathers and mothers who trod upon it entering into the house of God,—a sacred memento, and appropriately placed as one of the corner-stones of this Sanctuary.

Some thirty years out of the two hundred, the Church has been without a pastor ; one half of this period elapsed between the dismission of Mr. Woodbridge and the settlement of Mr.

Pierson, in which "their pulpit was supplied, for longer or shorter periods, by several occupants. Among these, Rev. Mr. Bayly preached in the years 1684-5; and in June of the latter year, a unanimous call was given to him to settle, at a meeting warned for that purpose, 'which was the number of twenty.' Another year passed without any permanent settlement being effected. When, in Sept., 1686, another vote was passed accepting his terms; still no settlement was effected. In 1692 the Rev. Mr. Mather was acting minister, and in August a call was given to him to settle. He continued to preach sometime longer but was not installed."

I have already stated that both Mr. Eliot and Mr. Mansfield preached nearly two years each, before becoming pastors by ordination and installation, but as the Church had previously given them a call to become such, I regard them as pastors from the beginning of their ministry here.

The average length of pastorates has been about fifteen years; and if we deduct that of Mr. Wood and Mr. Hine, which united amounted to only four years, it will bring the average up to a little over eighteen years.

Mr. Eliot's pastorate was the longest, being about fifty-six years; Mr. Hine's was the briefest, being one year and a half.

The annual additions to the Church were the largest during Mr. Foster's ministry, averaging almost seventeen; the smallest during Mr. Talcott's—being less than three annually.

There have been, including those now living, seventeen Deacons, fourteen of whom have finished their work, and have entered into their rest. They were men, generally, who were an honor to their office; and so far as they are remembered, were considered worthy, pious men, sincerely desirous of promoting the interest of religion and morality in the Church and community; inculcating, by their example, the duty of keeping holy the Sabbath day, which, with them, began with the going down of the sun on Saturday. Then all work would be suspended, and the time devoted to preparation for the duties of the coming day, and no little thing kept them from being *promptly* present, with their families, at the services of the Church. As sunset Saturday night began, so sunset Sunday eve closed the Sabbath.

Of the thirteen hundred and sixty-two, who have become members of this Church since its organization, one thousand, at least, have mouldered back to dust. Many of them are sleeping in yonder cemetery, among whom, as guardian shepherds, five of your former pastors keep watch—Pierson, Eliot, Huntington, Mansfield—the *youth winner*, as he was called,— and Foster, the devoted, but too early called.*

There, too, rests the tuneful Redfield, whose life was a speaking witness of the deep Christ-love, which, as a gushing fountain, lived within his soul. His loving words, his earnest prayers, his songs of praise,—these have written themselves upon your hearts ; and well do many of you remember the last time his faltering voice was heard, joining in with yours, in the closing hymn, as you went forth from the Sacramental Board.

Then, too, what *sweet* and *precious* memories cluster around the name of John L. Hull ; seldom heard, but always working for Christ ; whose daily life and consistent walk were fitting exponents of the living, loving, clinging faith, which made him what he was,—a devoted husband, an affectionate father, a kind neighbor, a good citizen and a worthy and *exemplary* Christian.

Let these two, whose memories are so fragrant and precious, be types of *many, many*, whose names I may not speak, who have here lived, and labored, and who, by a loving Father, have been taken from the Church militant, and are now the enrolled and rejoicing members of the Church triumphant.

During the two hundred years now gone, God has given many a gracious token of His presence. Time and again has

---

* The first Marriage, Birth and Death found recorded are the following :

" John Meigs and Sarah Wilcox were married the 7th day of March, 1665."

" Hannah, the Daughter of Joseph Wilcox, was born the 19th day of January, 1665."

" William Haydon died the 27th of Sept., 1669."

The oldest stone in the Clinton burial ground, has cut on it the letters " M. G." with the date 1670.

His Spirit been poured out upon this people,—glorious harvest times when many precious souls have been gathered into His Garner House.

How sacred, in the spirit life of this Church, should be the years 1711, '14, '21, '25, '31, '36 and 1757, in which Mr. Eliot, by the blessing of God, welcomed *more than five hundred to the Communion of this Church.* Yes, scattered all along through these two centuries, have been precious seasons of refreshing from the presence of the Lord, causing plants of righteousness to spring up and strengthen this vine of His love.

The last of these occurred in 1866, and was a beautiful illustration of the loving care of the Redeemer for His Church, as well as of the prophetic words, "He shall come down as rain upon the mown grass, like showers that water the Earth." With no pastor, and having no ministerial labor, save on the Sabbath, still the work went forward, quietly, yet with power, till more than fifty,—many of whom were from the Sabbath School,—were gathered, as precious fruit, into the bosom of the Church.

At some of the most prominent points in the history of this Church I have now glanced ; photographed, though dimly and imperfectly, its former pastors, of whom all, save two, have entered into their rest ; have spoken of the three Church buildings, which were but are nót,—which, together with this, have all stood on this very hill, and near the spot where this now stands ; called to mind the more than ten hundred, who, as we trust, have past on from here to the rest and joy of heaven ; and have reminded you of God's loving and watchful care towards you as a Church and people ; and now, as we stand here on this rocky, but oh, how sacred hill, and let our eyes glance back over the two hundred years to the birth morn of this Church, and behold what the world was then, and what it is now, we cannot but feel, and be deeply and movingly impressed with the fact, that they have been most important centuries in the civil, educational and religious history of the world.

Only forty-seven years had then past since our Pilgrim Fathers landed at Plymouth Rock,—yea, many were then living, who had been the subjects of Elizabeth, England's most noted queen, and some who had spent many a pleasant and never to be forgotten hour with the immortal Shakespeare.

Upon these shores the red man made his home,—here lived and died. Nay, our whole, broad, beautiful land was almost a howling wilderness. The vast, fertile prairies, where now stand mighty cities of rapid growth, and well cultivated fields are found, were then the Indians' hunting ground, untrodden by the white man, unexplored and unexplorable. Then we were the subjects of England. The thought of an independent, free government had not been conceived, much less born. In England the licentious Charles II was unvailing to the world his total depravity.

Only six years had past since Louis the XIV, to the State officials, who, at the death of Mazarine, his chief minister, had asked "to whom in the future they must address themselves on public business," had given this significant and ever memorable reply, "*To myself!*" Milton, the heaven-inspired poet, still lived, and, perchance, the out-breathings of his devoted heart may have brought down upon this then new born Church, the rich and life-giving blessing of that God whom he so loved. Peter the Great, who, in more senses than one, may be regarded as the father of the vast empire of Russia, was not yet born ; and William of Orange had not flooded Holland and thus repelled the invading hosts of France. Such a thing as a really free government was unknown. *It was an age of Despotism, when might made right.*

Since then what changes have taken place. What men have lived. What fearful scenes have been enacted. What glorious triumphs to human liberty have been gained. What fearfully bloody revolutions have swept over France. What untold horrors have been enacted in the Bastile. How has earth trembled beneath the excited tread of contending armies. All the battles of Wellington have been fought. Napoleon, inspired by the spirit of War, and impelled by the demon Ambition, has come, written his name in blood, and long since has departed from a startled, wondering, admiring world. The Inquisition, that hell-born instrument of death and torture,—worse than death,—has been forever banished.

In our own land, scenes no less wonderful and important have transpired. The events of the Indian wars have past.

The long seven years' struggle, put forth to attain our independence, with all concurrent events, has become, for these eighty years, part of the history of the past.

Liberty with us has become a reality ; and from a weak dependent we have grown stalwart and strong, so that to-day we grasp with one hand the turbulent Atlantic and with the other the milder Pacific, while the Arctic Ocean on the North, and the Gulf on the South, indicate our latitude. Well forged shackles have been broken, the enslaved have been set free, and we stand to-day a representative people. And not alone, for throughout all the nations of the world, the spirit of human liberty, emanating from us, is at work, so that to-day it is not the *man* but the *masses*, that rule.

Like wonderful transformations have taken place in the educational world, the results of which have filled lake, river, sound and ocean with floating palaces, steam-impelled ; spanned our country with railroads ; spread out like living threads, the electric wire, which with one swift bound leaps across the ocean, and will soon flash its messages around the world. Yea, results too great and grand to be grasped at once, have been attained since Pierson—ever to be honored name—became first President of Yale College.

If to-day he is permitted to look down upon us assembled here, where once he lived and labored, and with deep and anxious interest and steadfast hope, watched over and prayed for success of the then youthful College, and see it loaded with the thickly clustering honors of almost two centuries, already become America's *noblest* and *best* University, owning as her children more than *nine thousand*, who have gone forth from her various departments, who have proved, and are now proving in numberless ways, powers for good in the world ; and that holds, in her arms to-day, seven hundred young men, lacking one, that *one being equal to the number in the Senior Class in* 1702 ; if he is permitted from his distant home,—and perchance not so distant as we sometimes think,—to see all this, and the noble, learned and justly celebrated band of men that now have charge of its educational interests, and you,* its most

---

* President Woolsey was not able to be present on account of sickness, but Professor D. C. Gilman being his representative, he, (Pres. W.,) is addressed as though present.

honored head, sitting in the same chair in which he sat, while, like yourself, he was President of the College, then surely his spirit heart must glow, and his joy must receive a deeper thrill, as he beholds these *already* perfected results of his labors.

In the religious world, the change has been none the less marked. Freedom to worship God according to the dictates of one's own conscience, was a dream which few, even if any, hoped or expected would *ever* prove a reality. But to-day, no " Blue Laws" or laws of bigoted proscription mar or deface our statutes. Baptist, Methodist,—a name then unknown,—Episcopalian, or what not, may now, without let or hindrance, worship God. To-day, throughout the broad earth, no martyr stakes are erected ; no cruel flames, with their hissing, fiery tongues eat up the quivering flesh ; no instruments of cruel torture in the hands of heartless men, make life a curse, or force the heart to stay its beatings ; these are all things of the past, and *have become so* SINCE, ON THIS HILL, THE WATCH-FIRES OF GOD'S TRUTH WERE KINDLED.

Truth was walled out then ; now, the walls are broken down ; then, mankind were groping their way, seeing but dimly the way of life ; now, in fulfillment of Christ's blessed promise,—to draw all men unto Himself,—they have been lifted up into the purer atmosphere of a higher, holier life ; they see more clearly the truth—they better understand their real wants, so that from even Priest-ridden Italy, and lust-enslaved Turkey, comes the cry : " Send, oh, send us *Light and Life*,"—the Missionary and the Bible !

With all these revolutions in State and Church, with all the mighty changes in the civil, educational and religious world, this Church stands connected. Its life has formed a part of the great life which has existed around it. The spiritual influence which has gone forth from this sacred hill during the two hundred eventful years now past, has helped make the world what it is. The holy longings and the deeper pulsations of its inner life, have not only called down the blessings of God here, but have infused new life and power into His entire Catholic Church, so as a living branch of the true vine there is a fresher vitality here. Just as the rough, uncouth and stony surface of this hill, as it was two hundred years ago, has been wrought upon by the strong arm of man, and still stronger hand of time, till, compared with what it was, it is a beauteous lawn, dipping to the south and east and west, but with the same everlasting granite for its base, so, some of the rough points which may have marred the outer beauty of the Church here planted, have been brushed away by the changes of the past, but the same real spirit-life remains ; upon the same immovable, eternal *Foundation-Stone* she rests. Here, there is no change.

For one, I feel deeply grateful that God has given us this opportunity to celebrate the two hundredth anniversary of this Church,—a vine of His own planting,—that He has granted us this blessed, interest-fraught season to travel back over the past, and greet those who have gone on before us, and whom, ere long, we shall join in a never ending union.

And as I glance over the names of the under shepherds, who have been sent by God to watch and feed this flock ; when I contemplate the character of Woodbridge, the sterling worth of Pierson, whose efforts in behalf of education have been so wonderfully blest ; the intellectual power of Eliot, who was instrumental in gathering into the bosom of the Church more than five hundred immortal souls ; when in fine I call to mind the worth and work and character of those who have been pastors of this Church,—from Woodbridge to Moore,—I feel that you have reason to rejoice and praise God for his great and continued goodness to you as a Church and a people.

And as to-day, in our history as a Church, we *clasp hands with long ago, even as the green leafed 1867 reaches backward to the sere leafed 1667, and the verdant and smooth hand of the present clasps the dry and withered of the past, so with the hand of a living faith, let us, reaching upward and forward, clasp closely the hand of those who have gone before,* AND THUS, WITH ONE HAND IN HEAVEN AND THE OTHER ON EARTH,—ONE RESTING ON MORTALITY, THE OTHER GRASPING IMMORTALITY,—LET US PLANT OUR FEET MORE FIRMLY ON THE ROCK, CHRIST JESUS, *and like our fathers, as was their* *wont* at the settlement of each new pastor,* *solemnly renew our Covenant Vows, to live henceforth more to His glory, the building up of His kingdom and the gathering of immortal souls.*

---

* It was the custom of the early Fathers of this Church at the settlement of each new pastor to declare their "adhearance to the Doctrine of Faith and Covenant which were agreed upon and signed by our Rev. Pastor, the Rev. John Woodbridge," and others.

NOTE 2d.—The Cong. Church in what was then North, but now Killingworth, was organized in May, 1735.

THE ORIGINAL CONFESSION OF FAITH AND COVENANT OF THE CHURCH.

The Doctrine of faith, And the Covenant in and according unto which the Church of Christ at Kelinworth in the ffirst Imbodying of it was and yet is Ingaged unto God and their Duty.

I Believe that there is only one true, living, and Eternal God; infinite in his being, truth holyness, power, wisdom, justice and goodness distinguished into and subsisting in three glorious and undivided persons who are the same in substance, Essence & Attributes, equall in glory power and Majestie: yet distinguished by their Relative & personall properties. The ffather beeing the first in order & orignall, begetting the Son. The Son the second beeing begotten of the ffather. The holy ghost the third proceeding both from the ffather & the Son. That this God is the Almighty Creator, the sovercigne, wise and just upholder, desposer & Governour of all his Creaturs, & all their actions. That man being created after his Image, in a state of Integrity & Blessedness hath now suffered the Loss of both, by his disobedience to, and his disunion from God, and is by nature in a state of spiritual weakness, enmity, pollution, guilt unrighteousness & wrath.

I believe that when the fullness of time was come, God the ffather sent his true, only & eternall Son, true God and equall with the ffather to take upon him the nature of man, that so subsisting in and consisting of two distinct natures, & one undivided person, he might be a fitt mediator between, & reconciler of God & man; and an efficacious and sufficient Redeemer of man, by price and power, which Son of God being Anointed the King, Priest and Prophett of the Church, did execute his office by his obeying the Law, revealing the Gospell, suffering Death, and now presenting before the ffather his Righteousness, Death and merites, and in sending the holy spirit to inlighten, convince, call and sanctify all those that are given unto him, who, being enabled to believe in his name in the

Anniversary Hymn, written by Miss Wealtha Maria Hilliard.

Sung to the old Tune of "STAFFORD."

WE gather, in this Autumn time,
To offer notes of grateful praise
To Him whose goodness crowns the year,
Whose glories shine through endless days.

We praise Thee, that in counsels wise,
Of Thy most gracious, sovereign will,
Thou didst ordain this *Vine* to stand
Upon this consecrated hill,—

And that for these *Two Hundred* years
Thy never-tiring, loving hand
Hath nurtured it, caused it to spread,
And made it flourish in the land.

---

day when God, having raised them from the dead, shall judge all men according to their works, shall be adjudged to eternal life, and all others to everlasting punishment according to the scriptures of truth, which I believe to be the very word of God, and the only rule of faith & manners.

This God in Jesus Christ I avouch to be my God & do promise and Covenant to have no other Gods before him, but as his spirit & grace shall enable me I will believe his truths, obey his will, and run the Race of his Commandments, walking before him & beeing upright exercising my self in duties of piety towards God, sobrietie towards my self, & Justice and Charity towards others. And because Christ hath appointed spirituall administrations in his Church as the Sacraments to signifie, seale and exhibitt the benefitts of Christ, as also Admonitions for the unruley, censures for offenders, consolations for the penitent, teachings, quickenings, & exortations for all, I will truly countenance, & faithfully submit to the Regular dispensation of all in the Church of Christ in this place, and for the promoting of the same performe my injoyned & Respective duties unto others, that we may be all saved in the day of the Lord.

JOHN WOODBRIDGE,
EDWARD GRISWOLD,
WILLIAM HAYTON,
JOSIAH HULL,
HENRY FFARNAM,

And one hundred others " were Ingaged in the Covenant above mentioned before the year 1694."

We praise Thee, that thy love didst send
Thine husbandmen to train the *Vine*,
And that it prospered 'neath their care:
The glory, Lord, we own, is thine.

May every branch united be
To Christ, the true and living vine,
Till on each one the fruits of life
In rich, abundant clusters shine.

And when that fruit shall ripened be,
'Neath beams of God's perfecting grace,
He shall prepare, for each glad soul,
In realms of bliss, a welcome place,

Where, with the saints of ages past,
And all who yet redeemed shall be,
With Christ, our ever-blessed Lord,
We'll reign through all eternity.

BENEDICTION.

————•••————

At the close of this service, cordial invitations were given for all to visit the basement of the Church, where a sumptuous entertainment, provided by the ladies, awaited them. Some three hundred persons were bountifully supplied.

At this Thanksgiving Festival of the Church, her sons and daughters, with their guests, gathered around a table heaped with a liberal hand, with the best productions of a fruitful season, arranged with taste and skill. There were oysters, chicken pies, roast turkeys, chickens, ducks, roast pig, boiled ham and tongue; puddings, cakes and pastry, all looking as if they had come on purpose to grace this Thanksgiving Feast. The pumpkin pies were fully equal to the support of New England's ancient renown in that line, and the time-honored pork and beans were not forgotten.

Patient and skillful fingers had wrought many and curious devices in cake and pastry, among which the figures " 1667," and " 200," often appeared.

Boquets, arranged by Miss Marietta W. Hull, of the beautiful late blooming flowers of this region, adorned the tables.

Old friends here met, exchanging cheerful greetings. One tie binding all together, the remembrances of the past.

At two o'clock the audience reassembled. The choir giving the anthem, "*O! come, let us sing unto the Lord.*"

In response to a call from the moderator, Prof. D. C. GILMAN, of Yale College, (who had been seated in the old oaken chair which once belonged to Rector Pierson,) then made a short address, in which he described the early connection of Yale College with the town of Killingworth, and paid a tribute of respect to the first rector[*] of the " Collegiate School of Connecticut," the pastor also of the church now celebrating its two hundredth anniversary. He quoted a letter from Rev. Dr. Vermilye, of New York, referring to a silver tankard once belonging to the rector, which was for a while handed down from one generation to another as an heir-loom, but of which the trace, for the moment at least, has been lost. He remarked that Old Killingworth should be regarded by scholars as one of the shrines of American education, and promised to do what he could to secure a Memorial Stone, with a suitable inscription upon it, to mark the spot where the earliest senior classes of Yale College were taught.

He also mentioned that the Rev. Dr. Jared Elliot, successor of Rector Pierson, in the church, was like-

---

[*] Rev. Abraham Pierson.

wise a celebrated man, a graduate and trustee of the College, a physician and a scholar, the author of a treatise on Field Husbandry, and the friend and correspondent of Dr. Benjamin Franklin. We may presume, he said, that Franklin on his journeys from Philadelphia to Boston, took *the Shore Line Route*, like a sensible man, stopping at his friend, Dr. Elliot's, to talk over the scientific topics of the day.

Prof. Gilman expressed his regret that President Woolsey had been detained from this festival by ill-health, and in conclusion he urged the present generation to emulate the love of learning, the devotion to education, and the Christian virtues of those Worthies of the past whose services had been in the morning so fully recounted.

The next in order, was Mr. WM. L. KINGSLEY, Editor of the New Englander, whose theme was the patience and perseverance of the early settlers. He related a story illustrative of this.

A welcome guest was the Rev. JAMES D. MOORE. The sight of his face, and the sound of his voice, awakening tender memories in the hearts of many. He who for sixteen years had been identified with the interests of the Church, as its pastor, and who had given much time and patient research of the records of the past, was well prepared to speak of its early history.

He remarked that the storm of the preceding day, and the chilling cold of that, furnished fitting types of the trials and hardships* they endured, who here

---

* Killingworth, Dec. ye 20th, 1720:

*   *   *   *   *   *   *

Also it was agreed by voat that there shall be allowed 2*s*. per head for Every fox or wild cat that shall be killed within the town Bounds and to be paid out of the town treasurey, they that shall kill any fox or wild cat to bring the head thereof to the selectmen.

planted this "vine of the Lord," which had been such a mighty influence for good in all this region.

"There are two interesting facts connected with the original and the present names of this place. One is that Killingworth is a corruption of the first true name; the other is, that Clinton is the same name slightly varied. The name originally given to the place (upon passing from *Homonoscit Plantation* into a township) was *Kenilworth*, from a town in Warwickshire, England, from which place some of the first settlers are supposed to have come. In the course of a few years, we find by the town records, it came to be spelt *Kelinworth*, by the transposition of the *l* and *n*, doubtless in accordance with a similar change in the pronunciation. By the end of the century it became, by a horrible metamorphosis, *Killingworth*, which form (as evil, by a law of its nature, is persistent,) it still retains. The same change occurred in England, where the town in Warwickshire has in like manner become *Killingworth*.

When the south part of the original *Killingworth* was constituted into a new town, the name *Clinton* was chosen, in honor of Governor De Witt Clinton, like the long list of towns and counties of that name in the United States. It is unfortunate that the original name, *Kenilworth*, had not been selected, but as it was not, the name *Clinton* is the next best that could possibly have been adopted. It is, in fact, the *same name*. The first syllable, *Clin*, is manifestly only a slight change of the first corruption, *Kelin*, and the last syllable of each, *ton* and *worth*, have essentially the same signification, namely, an inclosure; *ton* or *tun*, in the old Saxon, was a fenced hill or fortification; *worth*, was a fenced place, a court, or castle. Making for the town a name full of meaning, with God's everlasting hills on the north, and the restless, murmuring sea on the south.

Nor does this identity of the names rest only on etymology. It is also proved by historic fact.

Kenilworth, England, was the barony of Sir Geoffrey de Clinton, chamberlain and treasurer of Henry the first, and who in the reign of Henry the second built there the famous Kenilworth Castle. It is most probable, therefore, that the name of the place (the fief,) was *Clinton*, or *Kenilton*, as these barons took title from the name of their barony. Hence, when Sir Geoffrey de Clinton built his castle, he called it *Kenilworth*, or *Kenilcastle.*"

The Rev. James A. Gallup followed Mr. Moore, and interested and amused the audience with a sketch of his "thoughts by the way." He had been wondering if this aged sister, who to-day was holding her *Two Hundredth Birthday Party*, would appear in the costume of *ye olden time*, with her cap and spectacles. If her voice would be faltering, her sight dim, her steps tottering with the infirmities of age. On the contrary, he had found that her bonnets were as fashionable, her eyes as bright, her form as erect and as full of the life and vigor of youth as her younger sisters. Might he not conclude that she had been the especial care of her Father, who had made her to be eternally youthful, beautiful, immortal.

Poem—Glimpses of the Years—written by Mrs. George B. Hilliard, and read by Mrs. Maria Josephine Warren.

GLIMPSES OF THE YEARS.

Friends, would ye look with fancy's gaze
Through the vista of Two Centuries?
Come where the Indian River flows,—
Where the red men paddled their bark canoes.
Here, in *later* times, the stately ship
Was built, and launched for the ocean trip;
Now, thousands of human beings ride
On iron rails, o'er its swelling tide.
On its grassy bank, which our fathers chose
A shrine for their sacred trust,
Our treasures rest in death's repose,
Dust mingling with the dust!
On the hill-top o'erlooking the river and lea,
The sparse settled hamlet, and blue, rock-bound sea,
Stands a monument, true to the faith of our sires,
The Church of their God, with its heaven-pointing spires.

See *here*, the foundations of time-honored Yale,—
And *there*, a stone school house, where old " Master TEAL,"
At the blazing hearth, with book on his knee,
Taught the children to say the A, B, C,
And showed the far-advanced, minister's *son*
How the intricate " Rule o' Three" was done.
But the Puritan's Church, with its large, square pews.
And very high pulpit, is long out of use.
Then, the pastor no gloomy "Shady Side" found.
His salary was paid in pork by the pound,
And wood, corn, and grain; cheese, butter, and flax ;
And a little "pin money" just settled the tax.
The Puritan mothers, with pious care,
Took thought for the minister's family wear.
In each donation basket with riches fraught,
The notable "skein o' yarn" was brought ;
Producing a fabric, the parish pride,
When a skillful hand the shuttle plied.
The red, low-roofed houses, with chimneys of stone,
And mammoth fire-places, are nearly all gone.
The architect copies their model no more,
Nor housewife, for carpet, strews sand on the floor.
They'd no marble-top tables, with books by the score,
But honored and blessed was their ancient lore,—
The Bible, and Psalm-book, and famed "Catechise,"
And "OLD SAYBROOK PLATFORM," so reverently prized.
No news-boy came, night, and morning, and noon,
With "New York Daily Times, Sun, and Tribune ;"
The news came, jogging along the post line
In saddle-bags, safe, but not always "on time."
Intelligence traveled at tardy rate,
Ere steam power and lightning came to compete.
But see! round the world on the wings of flame
Is borne through the darkness " *His wonderful name.*"
The vales are exalted, the mountains brought low,
And a pathway is found for the ransomed to go.
Hear! Earth's joyful millions respond to the thought
Sent *first* on the telegraph, " *What hath God wrought!*"

Singing,—" Guide me, Oh! Thou Great Jehovah."

The next speaker, LEWIS ELLIOTT STANTON, eloquently compared the privations of the past with the
privileges of the present. He said,—

" While listening to the Historical Discourse, I have been
thinking what curious changes have occurred in Clinton since
our ancestors came up to the house of God, upon this sacred
hill, at the sound of Samuel Griswold's church-going drum.

"What an unusual sight to witness, as the various household groups draw near the church. The head of the family, instead of carrying the light walking stick of to-day, is manfully shouldering his gun.*

"The pastor has alluded to the Class of 1702. What joys and sorrows, hopes and fears, must have concentrated upon that Senior Class of one! Who took the Valedictory? Who delivered the Latin Oration? Who carried off the Wooden Spoon? and who, I shudder at the inquiry, was the poorest scholar in that Class?

"You have spoken, sir, of Mr. David Redfield. But *you* never heard him sing. We remember how he made melody, with heart and voice, and many of us reflect upon the sublime and impressive words with which he invariably opened his prayer, 'O! Thou who art from everlasting to everlasting, the same unchangeable God.'

"Friends, how many of you have forgotten the old *Oak Tree* in the grave yard? The Bible says, 'Cursed be he who removeth his neighbor's landmark,' and I could almost pronounce a similar malediction upon any who should have cut down that ancient and revered landmark. Through many a generation it guarded the resting place of your ancestors; for the past few years withered, and with only a few leaves at the top, then leafless and dead; and the last time I saw it, the old tree had fallen, and lay among the graves, stretching bare arms to the sky. The sentinel oak is gone, and many of this audience have more friends who have been laid to rest under its branches than they have among those who are walking the earth in God's blessed sunlight.

"A good story is told of Dr. Elliot. He was careless of temporalities. His wife attended to them. The deacons paid him a quarter's salary one day. They were afraid he would give away the money. So they tied it up—none of our mod-

---

* August: 15: 1696.
At a meeting: the town thought it nescary to have a guard to attend the meting Saboth Days: they agreed and voted that if 8 men wold Appeer to attend that sarvice, they should have: 2: Shillings a pece allowed them in their town rate.

ern greenbacks, but good hard silver—in a silk handkerchief, in a great many knots. Going home, he met a poor woman, whose wants touched his heart. He tried to untie the knots, but the deacons' precaution proved too much for him. After working a while without success, he broke out with, ' Well, my good woman, I believe the Lord intends you shall have it all,' and handing over the handkerchief and silver, rode home to his prudent wife, with joy in his heart, but no money in his saddlebags.

"Eventful two hundred years ! 1667, the licentious era of the Restoration ; 1867, the era of liberty and peace, of new liberty for the slave, and of stable peace for all the people. ' *Qui transtulit sustinet,*' were, in 1667, words of faith and hope ; in 1867, they are words of assurance ; they illustrate the history of this Church and community. By the blessing of God, our ancestors wrought and conquered ; under the blessing of God, we inherit the fruit of their labors."

Mr. Stanton continued with a variety of local and personal anecdotes illustrative of the olden time, and the history of the Church and Town.

The Rev. Wm. E. Brooks desired to express his thanks for the experiences of the day, which had been signally blessed to him. Being comparatively a stranger, having been called to this pastorate but a few months previous, he had known little or nothing of the Church's history. But in making the preparations for the Historical Address, he had been compelled to delve into the old records, bringing out all the facts possible, until he had felt himself pervaded by a new and powerful affection for every thing pertaining to her life and growth. Happy in the thought that he had been called to work where such noble and efficient laborers had in their day and generation wrought. Pointing to the motto over the pulpit, he said,—

" This motto, that has been like a spirit of inspiration to me, and whose language of assurance we with full hearts can to-day adopt, may the future years as they come and go, prove still more especially ours. As we together go hand in hand down to the night of time, may there dawn for each one present, the morn of a blissful eternity."

Hymn, composed by Miss Wealtha Maria Hilliard.

TUNE—" *Old Hundred.*"

ANEW we gird the armor on;
 We grasp with firmness, faith, our shield;
Hope's helmet place upon our brow,
 And fain the Spirit's sword would wield.

We turn our faces to the foe;
 The hosts of sin come pressing on;
We fight not with the arm of flesh;
 By *love*, alone, the vict'ry's won.

We conquer in His mighty name,
 Who triumphed over death and hell;
What trophies in His name we'll win,
 Eternity alone can tell.

We'll march beneath the cross of Christ,
 Till our brief warfare shall be o'er,
Then wear the crown His hand bestows,
 And sing His praise forever more.

Doxology—sung as only an audience can sing, whose hearts are all alive with emotion—"Praise God, from whom all blessings flow."

Benediction by the Pastor.

www.ingramcontent.com/pod-product-compliance
Lightning Source LLC
Chambersburg PA
CBHW031759090426
42739CB00008B/1080